Copywrong
to Copywriter

Copywrong to Copywriter

a practical guide
to copywriting for
small businesses,
small organizations,
sole traders, and
lone rangers

Words by Tait Ischia

Illustrations by Jacob Zinman-Jeanes

SCRIBE
Melbourne • London

Scribe Publications
18–20 Edward St, Brunswick, Victoria 3056, Australia
2 John St, Clerkenwell, London, WC1N 2ES, United Kingdom
3754 Pleasant Ave, Suite 100, Minneapolis, Minnesota 55409, USA

First published 2016
This edition published by Scribe 2023

Cover and text design by Tristan Main
Illustrations by Jacob Zinman-Jeanes

Printed and bound in the UK by CPI Group (UK) Ltd, Croydon CR0
4YY

Scribe is committed to the sustainable use of natural resources and the
use of paper products made responsibly from those resources.

978 1 957363 30 1 (US edition)
978 1 922585 8 44 (Australian edition)
978 1 914484 73 5 (UK edition)
978 1 922586 80 3 (ebook)

Catalogue records for this book are available from the National Library
of Australia and the British Library.

scribepublications.com
scribepublications.com.au
scribepublications.co.uk

Thanks to Claire Feain, Tristan Main, Jacob Zinman-Jeanes, Mel Campbell, Penny Modra, and Stuart Geddes.

Contents

1.

YOU, THE EXPERT

You don't need a copywriter

Writing copy isn't an act of magic or surge of creativity. It's a logical process with tools and methods for achieving success. In that sense, copywriting is a job like any other. A professional copywriter must perform their job well, even when their creative spirit is still in bed, drooling on the pillow.

If you find the act of writing difficult, or have trouble choosing one word over another, it's possible to methodically develop your writing skills, write your own copy and make decisions about words with confidence.

The ability to capture bursts of creative energy, write lyrically and draw on vocabulary plays a relatively minor role in the end-to-end copywriting process.

The most important skill for a copywriter to master is an understanding of the decision-making process behind choosing one set of words over another and an ability to help their client through that process. If you get that far, you'll become a terrific copywriter.

Words that sell

While researching this book, I spent some time reading and listening to copywriting advice online. What I found bothered me.

Most advice focuses on helping you write 'words that sell'. While that may be the goal, I think trying to write this way is a distraction. The truth is, there are no words that sell – words can't magically convince a person to buy something. Sure, the hustlers and boardwalk salesmen of yesteryear fooled money out of people using words, but was that the secret to their success? Surely it was the ingenious methods of distraction and manipulation that convinced the passing crowds, not their choice of words.

Pick up any real estate brochure in your suburb and you'll see exactly what I mean. The imperative to write "words that sell" encourages real estate copywriters to remold small as "cozy", slightly larger as "spacious" and turn the possibly humdrum reality of your daily life into a much sexier sense of "lifestyle".

Which is fine. Some words are better to use than others. But I refuse to believe any word contains magical selling properties.

The truth is, successful real estate copywriting doesn't rely on choosing clever words. It relies on the strategy those words work to fulfill.

The smart real estate copywriter will enhance positive aspects of a house and conceal the negative – hoping to spark the imagination and emotion of buyers, while avoiding information that encourages uncertainty or insecurity.

The mistake many people make when writing copy is to focus on including clever adverbs, rather than developing a strong strategy. "Beautifully" appointed, "perfectly" situated and "superbly" crafted are common examples. These adverbs add color, but no new information. To be fair, it must be pretty hard to write anything truly original about these houses – after a while they'd all look the same. But surely writing this way only serves to make the reader more skeptical? At least I'm not willing to make any decisions about a house purely from reading a colorful description.

As you can probably tell, I'm not that kind of copywriter. I prefer to think of copywriting as the ability to write with clarity and authenticity about a subject I know well. Almost every copywriting job I complete relies more on my professional opinion about whether the writing says the right thing, for the right people, in the right way, than whether the words magically transform readers into adoring fans.

What readers want

Modern readers seek authenticity when interacting with organizations. Good grammar and clarity of message will do most of the work. The creative element is often just a glitzy sideshow, doing more for building a sense of personality and tone than for "converting prospects" – a term you'll hear from any sales or marketing guru espousing the must-know rules of copywriting.

When I'm working with small businesses, small organizations or single-person operations, my clients are generally embarking on a project to be taken seriously. They believe words will play a crucial role in that project, along with design and branding. If their customers take them seriously, maybe their customers will seriously contemplate spending their hard-earned cash on their special thing.

For readers to take you seriously, they want you to be honest and clear – and get to the point.

They don't want to be dazzled by an obtuse number of features, they don't want to be "sold", and they don't want to wade through information to get to what they want. If you spend the time to develop your strategy, and create your copy methodically, it's not difficult to get right. It just takes a little practice and determination.

Why are you here?

You're probably reading this book for one of two reasons: you're a business owner writing your own copy or you're an aspiring copywriter, hoping to become a professional.

If you're a business owner (or work for a small business), you've got it easy. You don't need to manage a client – you are the client. You know more about your area of expertise, and will have more insightful things to say than any copywriter will. Developing a strong strategy shouldn't take much effort at all.

On the other hand, if you want to become a professional copywriter, you'll need to learn to become an expert in someone else's business. The first step is to dive deep and to learn as much as possible – you should understand their business as if it is your own. When you're able to talk about another business from a position of confidence, creating a strategy and writing great copy will become a much simpler process.

And so it begins

After reading this guide, you'll be more confident making decisions about words. You'll be better equipped to write in an authentic tone of voice and address the needs of your audience, as well as to check for grammar and edit your work.

You may even be able to write copy without hiring a copywriter. Which doesn't bother me. The more confident and excited people feel about writing copy, the more pleasant it will become for everyone to interact with the world through the written word.

What even is copywriting? (Part one)

Copywriting is writing with an actionable outcome.

Regular writing makes you contemplate something.

Copywriting makes you do something.

How do you get someone to do something?

Ask them.

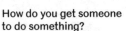

The call to action

Writing can be persuasive, but if you're not asking someone to do something, it's just writing.

The call to action is the secret ingredient. It turns regular writing into copywriting.

So what makes a good call to action?

Click here is a good one.

Find out more works too.

They're boring but they work.

Call now used to be popular.

I'm not sure it works these days. So don't use that one.

Enter your email is one of the best ones.

Point is, you don't need to be clever to be effective.

As long as you ask your reader to do something, you're calling them to action.

Then keep everything short and punchy.

You wanna smack them with clarity.

And that, my friends, is copywriting.

What even is copywriting? (Part two)

While writing with an actionable outcome goes some way to defining copywriting, there's a whole lot more lurking beneath the surface.

When someone first realizes they need a copywriter, they might have any number of services in mind.

They may be looking for web writing, journalism, scriptwriting, product naming, headlines, ad campaigns, concept development, user personas, information architecture, content audits, copy editing, proofreading or complex content strategies.

They might also require intricate knowledge about esoteric subjects, a sophisticated understanding of highly technical industries or years of experience in marketing, advertising, brand strategy or public relations.

A professional copywriter will have experience in almost all of these tasks, or specialize in one or two, and some will have sharpened their skill over many decades. So while the foundations of copywriting are simple, they quickly give rise to many complexities.

Luckily you won't need to learn any of these tasks to write copy. All you need to know is that writing with an actionable outcome links each of them. As long as you're the subject matter expert (as you most probably are), you're perfectly placed to write good copy that encourages your audience to take action.

But before you do, you'll need to develop your ability to write the right thing, to the right people, in the right way.

Over the next three chapters, I'll show you how to develop a strategy, find your voice, discover your audience and strengthen your writing skills through grammar.

By the end of this guide you'll have enough information to compile a comprehensive brief to begin the process yourself.

Complete the worksheet, start your brief

To make things easier, I've created a worksheet to use while reading this guide (see page 16). As you read each section, make notes and record any ideas.

Grab a pen and paper now. You never know
when you'll have a good idea. If you don't
record it, don't expect to remember it.

Once you've finished reading, you'll be able to tidy
up your notes and create a brief to either write your
own copy, or hand it over to a professional.

If you need, you can download the worksheet here:
http://copygui.de/worksheet

Strategy

① What are your objectives?

Begin with a shortlist. What do you want to achieve?
Keep them short. Be specific.

1. ....

2. ....

3. ....

4. ....   Now pick one:

5. ....

---

② What strategy will you choose?

Action	**Education**
Do you want your reader to:	Do you want your reader to:
☐ Make quick decisions	☐ Make an informed decision
☐ Find specific information	☐ Learn something new
☐ Scan your writing	☐ Think deeply
☐ Get on with their life	☐ Take their time

Voice

What is your tone of voice?

Do you want to sound authoritative, clever, witty, subdued, enthusiastic, weird, experienced, youthful?

Start by creating three separate tones of voice. When it comes time to start writing, it will be easier to find the right way to express your ideas.

Tone 1

....

....

Tone 2

....

....

Tone 3

....

....

The basics of an authoritative voice	1. Good grammar
	2. Don't fluff
	3. Find examples

Audience

(4) **Who are you talking to?**

Pick one person
It can be someone famous or someone you know

....

....

....

What do you want them to think?

....

....

....

What do you want them to do?

....

....

....

Audience

What is their context?

Physical mode

What is your reader doing while they're reading?

....

....

Cognitive mode

How much do they already know about your subject?

....

....

Emotional mode

How is your reader feeling?

....

....

....

2.

THE FUNDAMENTALS

The right thing: strategy and voice

In addition to writing with an actionable outcome, there's an equally important aspect running consistently through all facets of copywriting. It involves breaking the task down into two co-dependent sides of one system.

The first is strategy (objectives and purpose) and the second is voice (tone and phrasing). You can't have one without the other.

Strategy

Strategy is the set of choices you make when choosing what to write. It involves the goals and objectives you want to achieve and the facts and particulars you want your reader to absorb and act upon.

Voice

Voice is the words you choose, the length of sentences you construct and the elements of speech you add or leave out. These are the qualities that give your writing a unique personality.

Strong strategy + interesting voice = great copy

Great copywriting has a healthy balance of both strategy and voice. Something cleverly written but bearing no new information has a weak strategy. Something full of useful information but difficult to follow has a bland voice. When unique phrasing meets well-established objectives, you've stumbled on good, hard-working copy.

Let's begin with strategy

A strong strategy begins with a single, simple objective.

It can be as broad as "help our customers understand our product" or "make the reader like us".

It might also be specific, like "sell 100 copies of my book in the first week after launch" or "get that architecture studio I really love to hire me". Once you know what you're trying to achieve, it's much easier to write with clarity.

A word of warning: the easy part is thinking of objectives. The hard part is choosing one and sticking to it. Don't be tempted to dilute your strategy. List every objective you can, then prioritize one and one only.

If you're finding it difficult to pick an objective, just start writing. There are no wrong answers. Document your thoughts on the worksheet and write everything that comes to mind. You'll stumble upon a good starting point quickly.

Next, choose action or education

Most copywriting broadly falls into two categories: action and education. While both encourage your reader to take action, they do it in vastly different ways. It helps to know which side of the fence you sit on. The strategy you choose will determine the form your writing takes.

Action

Action is short and convincing. It sums up complex details in short spaces and encourages the reader to carry out a particular task. It features our old friend the "call to action", generally written as a short imperative sentence with a verb. (For instance, "Buy now" or "Join our newsletter".)

For more about sentence types, flip forward to page 60.

It gets to the point, quickly, so your reader can get on with doing whatever they came to do. It will probably feature headlines with short descriptions and may be used on the homepage of a website, an ad or a printed flier. It allows your reader to scan for keywords, find what they need, and take the logical next step.

Education

Education, on the other hand, is more subtle and in-depth. Its aim is to help the reader learn something new in order to make an informed decision. It has a similar objective to the call to action, but spends more time explaining rather than selling. It attempts to build trust and personality instead of outwardly encouraging the reader to take action.

Examples may include online writing such as periodic blog posts or in-depth case studies, as well as glossy printed publications produced by brands or organizations.

In a commercial situation, an education strategy works to remove any "perceived risks" a reader may have about making a purchase, particularly online.

"We knew that the key to true and sustained online success was removing any remaining risks the customer perceived through things like photos, videos and money-back guarantees."

—A large furniture retailer

If a reader establishes a long-term relationship with the writing an organization publishes, such as your own, they'll be more likely to take action when they're ready to make a commitment.

Make notes under the "action" and "education" headings on the worksheet. Will you need to choose one or a combination of the two? A homepage on a website might employ an action strategy, while another section might employ an education strategy.

Finding your voice

"hnnnnngngnngngngg"

Voice is the true expression of individual character. The best everyday example is the way you talk. The intonation of your speech, your choice of words and the subjects you choose to talk about are real-world expressions of your inner character. When you feel comfortable around others you speak freely and confidently. In this moment, others receive a clear sense of your unique personality and characteristics – in other words, your voice.

While voice is relatively easy to describe for our everyday speech, trying to define it as a component of professional writing is almost impossible. For this reason it can prove difficult for many people, especially those writing on behalf of a business or organization. Getting someone to feel comfortable about their writing voice can be as difficult as getting someone to feel comfortable about their image in a mirror.

The difficulties begin when trying to set boundaries for what a voice should or shouldn't be. Most businesses want a voice that is at once trustworthy and authoritative yet down-to-earth and easy to read. Which may seem like a reasonable request, but attempting to capture down-to-earth authority in a headline or short paragraph quickly becomes a challenge.

Don't let the uncertain rules of voice put you off. A confident and authoritative voice is easy to master with a few grammatical tricks and a little guidance.

The basics of an authoritative voice

Step one: Use good grammar

Writing with correct grammar and varied sentence length almost always creates a strong tone of voice.

Reading well-crafted words can feel as if the writer is inside your head, carrying on a conversation. It feels and sounds good. The sentences bounce around with rhythm. You understand clearly.

You needn't add any strange words, colloquialisms or extra fluff to add tone. It starts with good grammar.

Step two: Don't fluff

The worst thing you can do is say something without saying anything at all. It's an obvious sign that a writer has attempted to speak in a "tone of voice" but has failed to give the reader any information.

The rule is "Say it straight – say it great." If you describe what you're trying to say with clarity, tone will follow.

Example: This piece of writing manages to say a lot without saying much at all.

Coffee Culture
inside Brooklyn's bean belt

The Case for Coffee

There's a case for coffee and it's making its argument with visual boxes, giving shelf space to edibles – sweet and savory – leaving no dispute that their company is a welcomed food compliment to coffee. Within the coffee district of Park Slope, Windsor Terrace, and Prospect Heights, a few specialty coffee shops are just as concerned with creating a beautiful cup of coffee as they are with displaying what locals have with their coffee. This case for coffee highlights local spaces buoyed by area food artisans, chefs, and bakers. Peer closely, it's not stones being thrown, but smells of savory and sweet.

Step three: Find examples

If a tone of voice has resonated with you, there's a good chance it will resonate with others – particularly if you share characteristics with your target audience.

If you're not your target audience, find someone who fits your audience profile, then ask them for examples of copywriting they like.

Begin by identifying the words and phrases that stand out. Can you see a pattern? Is it the type of words used, the length of sentences, the cleverness, or the writer's understanding of the topic? If you can recognize what makes the tone engaging, you'll have an easier time finding a tone that suits you.

A short history of the professional writing voice

Since the 1970s, professional writers have been turning stuffy, formal documents into a tone of voice called Plain English. The aim is to remove big, clunky words packed with complex meaning and replace them with simple and brief words that anyone might understand. It's a movement that has helped countless brochures, forms and letters from your gas company read a lot easier, most of the time.

To really understand Plain English, it's important to understand the *registers* of language. At its most simple, there are three: formal, neutral, and informal. Plain English strives to be neutral, walking the line between the formal register of academia and bureaucracy, and the informal register of the schoolyard or the local bar.

But Plain English is not always the right tool for the job. When a reader needs to be convinced, not just informed, organizations will require more than the simple disinterestedness of Plain English. Something more like common street talk or slang, otherwise known as the informal register.

Back when the Plain English movement was beginning to make its way through the world of professional communications, the advertising industry was messing around with the informal register. They had very particular target markets in mind – teenagers, young professionals, mothers – and used in-jokes, colloquialisms and common sayings to "buddy up" with those they wanted to talk to. Getting on their level was seen as more important than talking in simple language that anyone might understand. Any marketer will tell you that using slang and street talk is a way to achieve empathy and lead to sales.

These days, modern marketers don't just aim to establish basic forms of empathy, they may also request copy that is less "sales-y". They use this term as an attempt to move away from common sales expressions, exclamations and unfounded claims in order to sound more authentic in their motivations.

Modern marketers also commonly request words that add emotion and force to their writing. These words are called "intensifiers", although marketers may not ask for them by name.

As the name suggests, intensifiers add degrees of intensity to writing – words like super, beautifully and awesome. While these words are a simple way to add tone to writing, they serve to pad writing with unnecessary clutter, and ultimately fail to add any new information, only "intensity".

Intensifiers can range from simple declarations of degree (such as very, so or really) to more extreme adjectives and adverbs (such as awesome, amazing or powerfully).

Where does this leave tone of voice? Which do we use and when? That's entirely up to you. The line between the informal, neutral, and formal registers is constantly changing and blurring.

The written language we use to communicate today has become more informal, particularly with the rise of the internet and social media. Readers seem to find the informal register more exciting and interesting, but may also be more skeptical of businesses and organizations that try to communicate in this way.

Above all, it's important to remember that if you write with clarity and honesty, and edit for grammar, you'll find yourself writing in an engaging tone of voice.

What an appropriate tone of voice can't mask, however, is a lack of understanding of a particular subject. Many would even argue that it doesn't matter how you write or the tone you use – as long as you convey an idea with clarity.

Write a brief for your tone of voice. Do you want to sound authoritative, clever, witty, subdued, enthusiastic, weird, experienced or youthful? Make some notes on the worksheet with the aim of creating three separate tones of voice. When it's time to start writing, you'll be able to try three different approaches, and pick the best one.

For the right people: audience

Only your reader can judge good writing and good communication. If your audience doesn't understand what you've said, you haven't understood your audience well enough. Good copywriting is about what's heard as well as what's said. It's your job to be able to hear the words you write the way your audience will hear them.

Problem is, most people find it difficult to think of target audiences outside the usual "25–35 Female" style of segmentation. Can you think of any women who were the same person at 25 as they were at 35? It seems illogical to think in these terms.

The "25–35" age and gender style of audience is a function of media and publishing companies that need to segment their audiences into large groups.

A magazine or television station will sell advertising space or airtime based on the age and gender of people who engage with their form of "media". This type of segmentation is a way to diagnose the media a company should buy. It won't help you to write with empathy or sympathy for a particular person.

A better way of approaching your audience is to imagine one person, preferably someone you know. It's important to be specific.

If you're targeting young couples buying furniture for their first house, think of someone who fits that profile. How do they talk? What are they into? What sort of computer do they use? Do they read much? What websites do they visit? What magazines do they read? It's much easier to imagine a real person than an abstract group of 25–35 year-olds you're almost certainly making wild, unfounded generalizations about.

Once you've got a real person in mind, you can create a user profile.

Creating a user profile

A user profile organizes your target person's characteristics into three simple, usable modes: Physical, Cognitive and Emotional.

Creating a user profile will help you better understand the needs of your audience at the moment they interact with your writing.

The physical mode

What is your reader doing while they're reading?

Are they sitting or walking? Are they watching the news or doing the washing? Are they on the couch or at a desk? How will these states affect the way they read?

> If they're on the go, keep things short and place clear calls to action in high visible areas. If they're on the couch after a long day, it may be okay to write something longer that requires a substantial time investment.

The cognitive mode

What is your reader capable of?

Are they familiar with the subject you're talking about or are they new to it? What is their reading level? What is their level of expertise? Will they need to understand complex concepts before they can make a decision or will they know what you're talking about straight away?

> If you know your reader already understands a lot about a particular topic, you won't need to explain complex concepts. If your audience is not familiar with a particular topic, try to talk in plain language and explain important concepts in simple terms.

The emotional mode

How is your reader feeling?

What is their emotional state? Are they stressed and busy or do they have time to learn and understand? How will their emotions affect their patience?

If your reader is stressed, best to keep things as straightforward and clear as possible. For example, if your audience is making an insurance claim, they'll want to know exactly what to do, and be able to make a claim quickly. If they're in a good mood with time on their hands, it's okay to play around – they're along for the ride.

Getting your audience to take action

It's no use attempting to write actionable copy without knowing what you want your audience to do.

Whether your copywriting is successful or not will depend on whether your audience behaves the way you want them to. What do you want them to think? What do you want them to do?

It may help to take the strategy developed in the first chapter and include it in your user profile.

It's much easier to measure the success of your strategy if you make it specific. A strategy like "build brand awareness" is too broad to measure. A better strategy might be "increase the number of enquiries through our online form". A strategy like this means you can set a goal and measure the outcome.

User profile example

Client
Simon's Organic Muesli

Project
Website homepage

Audience
Female, 30

Name
Simone

Physical mode
Sitting at home after work

Cognitive mode
Highly educated, sceptical of the hard sell,
knowledgeable about health food

Emotional mode
Tired, has had a busy day, but spending some
time online to wind down

Action/Education
Action

What do you want them to think?
"This muesli is the real deal. They have an answer to every question I ask about their muesli. They seem down to earth."

What do you want them to do?
Signup to our newsletter and request a free muesli sample

You can download this user profile by visiting
http://copygui.de/user-profile

In the right way: grammar

Most people seem to think of grammar as a large, mysterious collection of rules they never learned at school. The truth is that most writers are just as clueless about grammar – that's why they have editors.

When writing good copy, you don't need to know all the rules, just the important ones. They're extremely simple, easy to remember and apply. Don't let the weird, mathematical-sounding names (parentheses, contractions, conjunctions and so on) put you off. If your first language is English, most of this stuff will end up feeling so natural you'll find it obvious.

Use this section as a reference while editing. The more you practice, the better you'll get. Good grammar will always give your writing a strong tone of voice.

Active voice

A strong sentence places the "doer" of an action up front, before a verb or verb phrase. It's called the active voice.

The boy kicked the dog.

doer   verb   receiver

In the above example, the boy is the "doer" of the action. The dog is the one receiving the action.

A weak sentence places the "doer" away from the action, after a verb or verb phrase. It's called the passive voice.

The dog was kicked by the boy.

receiver   verb phrase   doer

Now the receiver of the action is at the front, while the actual "doer" has been relegated to the end of the sentence.

To quickly see whether a sentence is written in the active voice, ask whether the "doer" is up the front. If they're languishing at the end after the telltale word "by", you know you've got a passive sentence.

Try to make as many of your sentences active, if possible. They're shorter that way – and an active "doer" can make writing sound more honest and open.

Just remember, the active voice isn't the be-all and end-all. If the receiver is more important than the doer, there's nothing wrong with putting the receiver at the front of a sentence – it's still a grammatical sentence. Just make sure you're doing it for rhetorical effect, like this:

The dog was loved by everyone. The boy was not.

Other forms of active voice

In my experience, people respond well to writing they perceive to be "active", even if it's not attributable to the active voice. There seem to be two other grammatical tricks that produce a similar effect.

Imperative sentences

Many people perceive imperative sentences to be more "active" than other types of sentences. There are four different types of sentence: imperative, declarative, interrogative and exclamatory. An imperative sentence often begins with a verb and compels someone to do something. Sentences such as "join our newsletter", "make an enquiry" and "take a tour" are all imperative sentences. A sentence that states a fact but doesn't compel an action is a declarative sentence. Something like, "our newsletter is full of interesting news". Imperative sentences are almost always calls to action. That's why people perceive them to be "active". (See page 60 for more on sentence types.)

Beginning a sentence with an imperative

If you begin a long sentence with an imperative, it will sound more active. For example, the following sentence sounds passive because it takes too long to get to the action being compelled.

> For the latest news, advice and stories from our studio, filled with interesting tidbits and doo-dads, make sure you sign up to our newsletter.

The imperative, "sign up to our newsletter", didn't appear until the very end. It will sound more active written the following way:

> Sign up to our newsletter for the latest news, advice and stories from our studio, filled with interesting tidbits and doo-dads.

Commas

Use commas sparingly. Your copy will be punchier, more authoritative and clear. If that's all you remember about commas, you'll be a great copywriter.

The more commas you add to a sentence, the more your reader will need to carry in their head, and if the sentence continues any longer than it should, it might be difficult to continue reading, or remember what the very first thing you wanted to communicate was, or lose their train of thought altogether.

If you must use commas (which is almost certain) the rules get difficult fast. For this reason, I'm going to spare you the lesson and provide a list of things to look out for instead.

Becoming an expert in comma usage requires knowledge of participial phrases and appositives.

You'll need to understand what makes a run-on sentence, how to avoid the comma splice and how to avoid splitting a subject from its verb. All of these lessons are just a Google search away.

You'll also need to learn parenthetical sentences. But don't jump on Google just yet, I'm going to explain them next.

Many people say Ernest Hemingway was a brilliant writer for his efficient and restrained use of commas. This isn't entirely true; he often wrote incredibly long, comma-filled sentences. But for better or worse, the tag has stuck.

Now you can compare yourself to Hemingway using a free online application. Just paste your writing into Hemingway (the app, not the person) and it will rate your writing based on the length of your sentences and choice of words. It's a great way to get instant feedback on your writing.

http://www.hemingwayapp.com/

Parenthetical sentences

One of the best ways to improve your grammar, and use commas well, is to use parenthetical sentences. They sound difficult but are incredibly easy to understand and apply.

A parenthesis is just a fancy word for a bracket. A parenthetical sentence (like this one) includes a bracketed sentence in its middle. Instead of using brackets, which look very odd, replace them with commas. Just like the last sentence.

If you feel like you're likely to use too many commas, reduce your sentences into easily digested parenthetical sentences. They're much easier to read and give your writing a natural flow. They'll also help if you're ever unsure where to put your commas.

You know you're doing it right when you can take away the bracketed phrase and the components of the sentence still make sense (when "making sense" is defined as "having a verb, a subject and an object").

Tense

There are three tenses: past, present and future.

Past: It happened yesterday.
Present: It's happening right now.
Future: It will happen tomorrow.

It's simple stuff, but you'd be surprised how easy it is to slip between tenses while writing. Try editing while looking purely for changes in tense. You might find you've slipped in and out by mistake.

> There are actually more than the three tenses mentioned above – there are twelve. It starts to get very complicated very quickly; past perfects tangle with future perfect continuous-es, making editing a real mess. As long as you keep your -ed, -ing and -en suffixes consistent, you have little to worry about.

First, second and third person

Should businesses write in the first, second or third person? I get asked this question a lot. The answer is a little bit of everything.

> First person: We
> Second person: You
> Third person: Simon's Organic Muesli, It

Try to use "we" instead of your company name and "you" instead of "the customer" or "the reader".

Bad example

Simon's Organic Muesli is proud to use the best local wheat producers. It is part of our commitment to providing our customers with the finest ingredients.

Good example

We are proud to use the best local wheat producers. It's part of our commitment to providing you with the finest ingredients.

Using "we" (the first person) is a great way to set a casual, no-nonsense tone. Using "you" (the second person) is a great way to put the reader in the picture.

Most of your copy should probably use the we/you combination. It helps to bridge the gap between organization and reader, as if you're talking one-on-one. It also invokes the power of inclusive language, an incredibly useful tool for getting the reader to invest emotionally (or financially) in what you have to say.

The only exception is when writing a standard "about" or "bio" style introduction about a company or person. In this case, use the full name the first and only time. When someone types the name into Google, it will show up in a Google search.

Good example

> Simon's Organic Muesli uses the best local wheat producers. It's part of our commitment to providing you with the finest ingredients.

When writing for the web, the best place to put this copy is in the "meta description" – part of the page metadata used by Google to display search results. The meta description appears under the URL in a Google search.

Simon's Organic Muesli
www.simonsorganic.com
Simon's Organic Muesli uses the best local wheat producers. It's part of our commitment to providing you with the finest ingredients.

When writing about your company, beware the "corporate plural". An organization name, like "Simon's Organic Muesli", is singular, not plural.

Although you might use "we" (a plural pronoun) in order to refer to "we the team at Simon's Organic Muesli", when referring to the organization name make sure you use singular modifiers (the word you put directly after the name).

For example, "Simon's Organic Muesli is" instead of "Simon's Organic Muesli are". Or "Simon's Organic Muesli provides" instead of "Simon's Organic Muesli provide".

If you find it difficult to tell your singulars from your plurals, swap your own name in place of the organization's. If it sounds right with your name instead, it's probably singular.

Contractions

It's often said that contractions – words shortened with apostrophes – make writing more informal.

People love to use the longer versions because they believe it adds an air of formality to their writing. There's something about "cannot" that "can't" cannot convey.

Personally, I prefer contractions. They make the reading experience flow better. Unless you're writing a thesis or legal letter, it's okay to use contractions. It really helps to remove the stuffy authoritarianism from your writing and give it a friendly tone.

Having said this, some contractions are better to use than others. Not all contractions were made equal. The important thing to consider when using a contraction is its commonality. "It is", "do not" and "cannot" are all commonly contracted down to "it's", "don't" and "can't".

On the other hand, "I will" (I'll), "I have" (I've) and "have not" (haven't) are a little trickier. They're borderline cases where the informality of the contraction is probably just a little too prominent. It's best to use these contractions with caution.

Then just avoid writing "should've", "could've" and "ain't" altogether, unless it's a deliberate decision you've made to express character.

Idiom

Because our brains are lazy and work in mysterious ways, we often resort to popular figures of speech, otherwise known as idiom, instead of speaking plainly.

Commonly used idioms include "piece of cake", "spot on" and "put you on the right track". They can be very useful, particularly in copywriting, to make your tone of voice more conversational and casual. But be careful. If used too often, they'll make your writing feel vague and abstract. Try to remove common figures of speech in your writing and replace them with plain language.

Instead of "it's a piece of cake", try "it's simple".

Instead of "you'd be spot on", try "you're right".

Instead of "put you on the right track", try "make it easier for you".

If you're struggling to find a simple way of expressing an idiom, look it up on Google. There are lots of helpful resources that'll "put you on the right track".

Sentence types

There are four sentence types: declarative, imperative, interrogative and exclamatory. Understanding the usefulness of sentence types will often come in handy when copywriting, particularly when writing headlines.

If you're attempting to find the right headline for a given situation, try the same sentence written in each of the four sentence types.

The imperative is almost always the simplest way to express a headline – particularly when you're asking the reader to act.

Declarative: Our newsletter is cool
(Making a statement)

Imperative: Join our newsletter
(Commanding someone do something)

Interrogative: Would you like to join our newsletter?
(Asking a question)

Exclamatory: Join our damn newsletter!
(Expressing an emotion)

Nominalization

Nominalization can change the tone of your writing instantly. It's magic.

Most commonly used in academic writing, nominalization works by changing verbs (actions or events) into nouns (things or concepts).

For example:

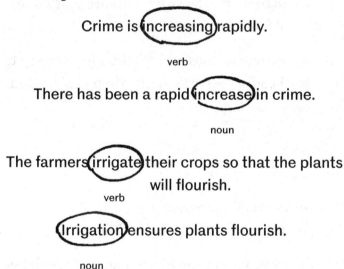

Crime is (increasing) rapidly.

verb

There has been a rapid (increase) in crime.

noun

The farmers (irrigate) their crops so that the plants will flourish.

verb

(Irrigation) ensures plants flourish.

noun

Nominalization is most commonly used to give writing a sense of objectivity. By removing the action words (verbs), it can sound like you're a detached observer rather than an overly invested salesperson.

But be careful: removing action words can also make your writing sound empty and lifeless. For this reason, nominalization is sometimes accused of creating "zombie nouns". If you're going to use it in your writing, make sure it's for the right reasons.

If grammar is something you'd like to know intimately, stop hunting around online and buy a good grammar book from one of the big dictionary publishers.

Oxford and Collins both publish great books that address the full complexities of English without making it confusing. There are also other great books about voice and tone, as well as thick rulebooks covering the finer details of word use. I have a copy of each of the following on my desk at all times:

Grammar

Improve Your Grammar (Collins)

Everyday Grammar (Oxford Paperback Reference)

Voice and tone

The Elements of Style by William Strunk Jr and EB White ("Strunk and White")

Spunk and Bite: A Writer's Guide to Bold, Contemporary Style by Arthur Plotnik

The Subversive Copy Editor by Carol Fisher Saller

Style manuals

Style Manual (Australian Government), http://stylemanual.gov.au (Australia)

The Chicago Manual of Style, 17th Edition by University of Chicago Press (United States)

The Guardian and Observer Style Guide, http://theguardian.com/guardian-observer-style-guide (United Kingdom)

3.

GET TO WORK

Writing for the web

The internet has been both a blessing and curse for copywriting. While there have never been so many people reading the written word, they're infinitely more impatient. Most scan for keywords and only read what's relevant to them. Some don't read at all – they usually want to complete a task as quickly as possible, forget they've just spent $300 on something they shouldn't have, and then get onto reading mind-numbing articles about celebrities.

In order to stand out from the crowd and make your copy consumable by short attention spans, there are a few crucial things to keep in mind.

Keep decisions to a minimum

If you give the reader too many choices on one page, they're bound to make none.

What's the most important thing you want the reader to do once they've read the page? Give them as few choices as possible.

Imagine your website is being viewed by people in a hurry or with short attention spans. We'd love to think our website is viewed by patient and focused readers, but mostly they're in some sort of rush, so keep it short.

Use a clear page hierarchy

If you're writing copy for a webpage, it's very important that the reader knows how to order the information on the page from most important to least important. They're probably making decisions based on a quick, impatient scan.

If there are ten things you want your audience to know, list them out in order of importance. Work with a designer to make sure the size of typography, placement of copy, any images and calls to action reflect your order of importance.

The scrollbar is your best friend

Books that are impossible to put down are commonly called "page-turners". A page-turner works because the writer has set up a question only answerable by turning multiple pages. It conceals juicy information you won't discover unless you keep reading.

The scrollbar (the "bar" in your web browser that allows you to scroll up and down the webpage) has the same effect. If you're publishing a long article on a webpage, set up the narrative first, and then reveal parts of the story as the reader scrolls. Thinking this way works just as well for homepages with a few headlines as it does for long articles.

"The fold" does not exist

The reason you can build a narrative using the scrollbar is because people love to scroll. It's usually the first thing they do when they arrive at a website. It's also a very good argument against the existence of "the fold".

"The fold" is a term borrowed from newspaper design. When newspapers are laid out on a stand, they're folded in half, revealing the information on the top half of the front page only. It means the information included "above the fold" has to grab a person's attention; otherwise they might not buy the newspaper.

But this isn't how people view websites. Not only do people scroll as soon as they land on a webpage, they might also be using a very large screen, small laptop screen or mobile phone, each of which have vastly different heights and widths. For this reason, it's impossible to know what information is above or below the fold on any particular screen.

> Don't try to cram the most important information above an imaginary "fold". Pace information out vertically and encourage your reader to use the scrollbar.

Get the basics of SEO right

SEO, which stands for Search Engine Optimisation, is an acronym thrown around regularly. It's so hotly discussed because it marks the crossover from listing a business in the Yellow Pages directory to our modern style of searching for a business on Google.

Most SEO companies will tell you they can help you rank higher on Google. While this is possible, it's not something a consultant will be able to manufacture for you in an afternoon. It can be a complicated, painstaking, and expensive process.

Luckily you can do a lot yourself. The devil is in the detail. Get the structure of your site organized, clean, and clear, as well as the underlying metadata. It can take some work, but it's worth it.

Optimizing your search results then falls into three broad tasks: writing things that people find interesting and useful, using keywords strategically throughout your website, and getting other popular sites to link to yours.

Useful and interesting writing

Google is one of the biggest companies on the planet, and its search engine is the jewel in its crown. Their developers have spent a lot of time and energy perfecting the search algorithm. Their mission has been to provide users with the most useful and relevant information based on the collection of words typed into the search box.

For this reason, their algorithm promotes pages and websites it believes are truly useful to people and downgrades the ones that are not. If you focus on consistently publishing engaging content, you will be rewarded. This is by far the most substantial thing Google looks for when deciding whether to rank your page highly or not.

Use keywords strategically

How do you make your content useful and interesting? By targeting keywords.

When someone types a word or phrase into Google, they expect pages that answer their specific question, using the words they've typed. Your job is to try to decipher what these words and phrases might be, then to write pages that answer them in a useful and interesting way.

But Google doesn't just look for instances of words; it looks for the connection between instances. Your page will rank higher if a keyword has been used consistently in several different elements of the page content.

Just be warned: this does not mean you should litter your keywords anywhere and everywhere. Using a keyword once in the URL, once in the page title, once in the meta description, once in the heading, once in the alt text of any image, and then two or three times in the body text will be enough to let Google know this is a high-quality page about your chosen keyword.

Get other popular sites to link to yours

The third major factor Google considers in its algorithm is called "backlinking". A good backlink score means there are lots of other, important websites that link to yours. This may mean popular blogs, news sites, news aggregators or any other website. The more people who come to your site from popular places, the higher your "PageRank" (the ranking your page gets in a Google search) will be.

The best way to get other people to link to you is to have really good, original content – like photography, videos or writing on your website. People love to write about these things on news sites and blogs and share them with their friends.

Don't be tempted to game the system. The sneaky tricks and workarounds used by shady SEO characters are frowned upon by Google and popularly known as "black hat SEO". These techniques include keyword stuffing, doorway pages, invisible text, blog spam, comment spam and link farms. If you don't know what any of those things are, you'll have no trouble avoiding them. Google penalizes websites found to employ any black hat SEO techniques by removing them from their search results.

Google is the best search engine for a reason. It has complex algorithms that outsmart human trickery. If you write for humans and follow Google's simple guidelines (and don't try to trick the machines), your content will naturally find its way to the top of the Google pile.

The official word from Google:

"Website owners who spend their energies upholding the spirit of the basic principles will provide a much better user experience and subsequently enjoy better ranking than those who spend their time looking for loop-holes they can exploit."

For more information, type "google seo starter guide" into a Google search, and read Google's official advice.

The clickbait debate

If you type "copywriting advice" into Google, most of what you'll find refers to a technique called "clickbaiting".

Clickbaiting plays on our innermost desires, manipulating our procrastination muscle and rendering it almost impossible not to click a link our rational brain might normally reject.

POPULAR OFFERS

 Cut down a bit of your belly each day with this 1 tip …

 Stay At Home Dog Makes $5,000 a day with Weird trick

 The Trick to Turning into Ephemeral Mist REVEALED!

 Read the mandatory dating advice you must follow to have a successful relationship

The basic technique in clickbaiting is to withhold the object of the sentence. For example, the sentence "cut down a bit on your belly each day with *this one* tip" impels the reader to click the link to discover the "one tip". Couple this dubious weight-loss claim with a picture of an attractive woman and you've got a standard clickbait link.

There are many companies attempting to trick readers and inflate their site statistics using clickbaiting techniques, just like the example above. It's also becoming a ubiquitous trend within journalism aimed at increasing advertising revenue.

Clay Shirky, a prominent American journalist and critic, says that journalism has two imperatives: to be truthful and to be interesting. He also adds, "Almost everything that's true is boring and almost everything that's interesting is false."

Shirky says that while journalists are expected to be truthful, they are rewarded for being interesting. And as such, the motivation to be rewarded for publishing something interesting will outweigh the benefit of publishing something truthful.

Clickbait is an easy shortcut to interesting. It gives readers an extra reason to read an article, even if it may not have interested them in the first place.

When it comes to copywriting, shortcuts rarely produce results. Attempting to play on the lizard brain of lazy internet users may boost your site statistics in the short term, but it's bound to leave your customers or clients feeling either short-changed or unimpressed in the long term. Build your brand by writing with clarity and purpose, not by treating your readers like dummies.

If you're having trouble getting people to click links in an email newsletter or a Google ad, test different headline techniques and try to find something that works. Try clickbait techniques, sure, but also try SEO keywords, clever puns, funny headlines, juxtaposing your writing with a picture or being as factually correct as possible. The point is to try lots of solutions until you find something that works.

There is no silver bullet for getting people to click links on the internet. Clever headlines don't always work, and sometimes seemingly boring and straightforward headlines do. If you test, learn and adapt, you'll find the right solution for the job at hand.

How to start writing

The worst, most difficult, most frustrating part of writing is the beginning. You might start, stop, and start again, metaphorically scrunching page after page and dumping the attempts in the trash icon. It's like a writer and an editor are inside your mind fighting over small, dumb, inconsequential things, and neither seems to be winning.

This is normal when you're starting out. The way around it is to have a strategy – and when that doesn't work, to try another one.

Strategies for starting

List keywords

Write down as many words as you can. They don't need to be in sentences; just list single words. Discuss with someone else the meaning and tone of the words you've chosen. Which ones feel right? Which ones don't? Once you have a good idea of what works, you can begin to write.

Free write

Don't try to write perfectly from the start. Write
a page full of thoughts, ideas, bad sentences and
disconnected ramblings. Don't censor yourself,
don't fix grammar, and don't delete anything. Fill
a page and see if something sticks. Some writing is
better than no writing. Once you've got something
to work with, you can begin piecing it together. It
may have nothing to do with what you're trying to
say, but that doesn't matter. Let it all out.

Make a plan

List the main arguments you want to communicate
and the keywords you want to use. It doesn't need to
be detailed – a short bulleted list will suffice. Add some
of the arguments and thoughts you developed from
free writing as well as any keywords from your list.

Write hot, edit cold

Once you have a plan, you can begin writing.
To make sure you don't get bogged down editing as
you go, it's a good idea to "write hot, edit cold".

Writing hot

The plan is to keep writing without stopping. Resist the urge to edit as you go. If you don't like what you just wrote, don't delete it. Keep moving. Some authors will write whole chapters only to throw them in the bin at the end of the day. Winston Churchill once said, "When you're going through hell, keep going." He wasn't talking about writing, but for the sake of this task, let's pretend he was.

Editing cold

Once you've written a first draft (or as much as you can handle in one sitting) put the writing away, do something else for a while, and return later to begin editing. It doesn't matter if it's ten minutes, one hour or a day: editing later makes it easier for your analytical brain to address any structural or grammatical errors with objectivity.

Write in a different tone of voice

If you've been writing and editing and you're still not entirely happy with the outcome, try rewriting your copy in three or four different tones of voice. You could write one straight and serious, and then try another that's more humorous. You might try one that uses a negative tone, and another that's overly positive. You might even try one without pronouns. Once you've finished three or four versions, discuss the results with someone else. What works and what doesn't? You'll get a good idea pretty quickly.

Read it aloud

If a piece of writing has good rhythm, it'll be easy to read out loud, and the flow between ideas will seem logical and natural. If something doesn't feel right, write it again until it works when you read it to yourself in the privacy of your lounge room. It's a great way to fix any issues you missed during editing.

Developing a brief

The most important part of the copywriting process is writing a good brief. Never start writing copy without one.

By this stage you'll have downloaded the worksheet (**http://copygui.de/worksheet**), filled out each section, and have a page full of great information to work with. Now's the time to use your editing skills, pick the best bits and create a final version.

> Try to keep your brief to one page. (They call it a brief for a reason.) A short and clear brief will produce better copy.

Depending on your strategy, you might produce one brief or several. When working on large website projects, some organizations will create a single brief for every new page of copy to be created. It could mean hundreds of briefs.

The more planning you put into deciding what you're going to say – and to whom and in what tone of voice you're going to say it – the stronger and more effective your copy will be. It will also make it a lot easier to make decisions about words and choose the words that are right for the job.

Download the brief template

To make writing your brief as simple as possible, I've created a brief template with every important section you need to complete.

http://copygui.de/brief-template

Example brief

Client
(*That's you!*)
Simon's Organic Muesli

Project
(*Give the project a name*)
Website and ecommerce store

Background
(*Write down everything you know about this project*)
Simon's Organic Muesli began in 2007 when Simon decided to start making muesli from his kitchen. In the years since, he's begun selling muesli in local supermarkets and employs two people.

Demographic
(*Add all the information from your user profile*)
Female, 30

Name
Simone

Physical mode
Sitting at home after work

Cognitive mode
Highly educated, skeptical of the hard sell,
knowledgeable about health food

Emotional mode
Tired, has had a busy day, but spending some
time online to wind down

What do you want them to think?
"This muesli is the real deal. They have an
answer to every question I ask about their
muesli. They seem down to earth."

What do you want them to do?
(*Use one of the objectives from your strategy*)
Signup to our newsletter and request a free
muesli sample

Is your strategy "action" or "education"?
Action

Tone of voice
(*List the three tones of voice you decided earlier.*
Or if you know what you want, list one only.)
1. Positive, casual
2. Dramatic, honest
3. Quirky, off-beat

Now you know a thing or two about copywriting

But nobody expects you to be an expert.

Like any skill, you need to practice. Which just means writing, drafting, editing and more writing. That's the best thing about copywriting – you can chip away until it works just the way you want.

The point of this guide isn't to make you an expert. At least not yet. It's to give you the tools to be more confident making decisions about words and begin writing with a clear strategy for your business or organization. So if you take anything away with you, be confident about copy. Be confident about what you're saying, be confident about your voice and be confident about your audience. Clarity and tone will follow.

Then all you need to do is review your writing at various stages of the year. There's nothing worse than out-of-date information.

Finally, remember that copywriting will only ever be one aspect of your business, organization or brand. In most cases it'll only be a small one. Have fun, be honest about what you've got to offer the world, be bold and try something new. Even if it breaks every rule in this book.

Checklist

Developing a strategy

☐ Decide on a single, simple objective
☐ Choose an action or education strategy

Voice

☐ A strong voice begins with good grammar
☐ Don't fluff
☐ Find examples
☐ Choose three tones of voice for your brief

Audience

☐ Pick a single person, preferably someone you know
☐ What do you want them to do?
☐ Create a user profile (physical, emotional, cognitive)

Grammar

☐ Active voice
☐ Commas
☐ Parenthetical sentences
☐ Tense
☐ First, second and third person

- ☐ Contractions
- ☐ Idiom
- ☐ Sentence types
- ☐ Nominalization

Writing for the web

- ☐ Keep reader decisions to a minimum
- ☐ Use a clear page hierarchy
- ☐ The scrollbar is your best friend
- ☐ The fold does not exist
- ☐ Get the basics of SEO right
- ☐ Avoid writing clickbait

How to start writing

- ☐ List keywords
- ☐ Free write
- ☐ Write hot, edit cold
- ☐ Try a different tone of voice
- ☐ Read it aloud

Later

- ☐ Have another look at your copy
- ☐ Has any information changed?
- ☐ Does it need a refresh?

Index

Notes

....

....

....

....

....

....

....

....

....

....

....

....

....

....

....

....

....

....

....

....

....

....

....

....

....

....

....

....

....

....

....

....

....

....

....

....

....

....

....

....

....

NOTES

....

....

....

....

....

....

....

....

....

....

....

....

....

....

....

....

....

....

....

....

....

....

....

....

....

....

....

....

....

....

....

....

....

....

....

....

....

....

....

....

....

....

NOTES